Cshantay Publishing
ISBN 978-1-7321319-7-2
Copyright 2023

Daughter of the Culture

by

LaShonda C. Henderson

Radical Prose

Conversation

And

Action

For my people, because you made me, and I love you for it.

Family Cycles

We forget about the role cycles play in our
lives, if you'd pay attention, you'd see
predictable behavior from people.
My son says, "you don't predict the future
Mom, you're accurate in your study of
human behavior, you make sound
conclusions to stay safe."
But I'd tell you, think of a daughter who
loves her Daddy. Watch to see if she'll
ignore her mother's tears to comfort him,
even if he's the source of pain. If he smiles
enough when she goes to him, if he's calm
when he sees her face, she concludes that
no other woman can soothe a man
properly but her.
Think of a son who loves his
Momma. Watch to see if he'll never look
at his father's face when she goes off, he
just follows instructions. If she rewards
his obedience, his loyalty to her, he
concludes that no other man can soothe a
woman properly but him.

They both, boy and girl, develop savior
complexes.

It is important to note that no parent is aware of how their every move is being watched and mimicked. No parent can make perfect decisions all day every day. But I'd caution, the drama shown to children as normal, becomes their ordinary lives, and it's important to note that love you show becomes ordinary too.

Wealth, generational COIN
is teaching, explaining why you do what you do, so children can repeat the cycle or become empowered to choose another path.
There are no villains in our stories, only people trying to fortify their storehouses, to prepare for bouts of famine, so they can grab love from the shelf whenever they need it.
Show us how to do that, dear members of our society, do it for the culture, cradle to grave!

■■■■■■■■■■■■■■■■■■■■■■■■■■■■■■■■■■■

Conversation:

It is important that you ask your parents questions about the choices they make. During a heated argument, is not one of those times that questions should be asked either, I mean when you are in the middle of being punished for doing something that violates their rules. By understanding why your parents think, act, and make choices, you can learn up close and personal a method of making choices too.

■■■■■■■■■■■■■■■■■■■■■■■■■■■■■■■■■■■

Action:

You may not know you are repeating a cycle. But you do become what you see.

Begin by asking yourself:

Are my parents, peers, or elders upset because they know the outcome of my action? Should I ask them during a quiet time about what happened when they made a choice in a situation my own? What can I do with the information shared to improve my life?

Banker Rules

I practiced loving, not random musical
chairs loving either. I studied and said,
"I'd like to experience that type of love."

So I did

I'd love, then pull back to see if love was
reciprocated. No one wants love to
become a burden to anyone else. If it was
reciprocated, I gave more, shared more of
myself, opened my safe places for
observation.

Undisciplined men would say that was
teasing, men with understanding would
praise my Father, Daddy, and Uncles for
teaching me to cover myself properly.

There was a time when a dowry was
demanded, I think it was wise.
Because no man would be in multiple
women's faces if he had his life savings
invested in the union.
He'd be a lot more cautious about who he
was with, I mean if he embarrassed her or
her family before he married her.

I mean if he knew he'd lose his investment, if what he chose was no longer available to him because of his own behavior, I KNOW he'd put childish things away.

Men who give nothing never fear losing the nothing they put in.

They thrill ride daughters.

Consider love from the eyes of a beloved daughter, so you can discover the truth, I mean put the energy out you want to receive, and by demonstration, help others call themselves home to their own heart.

Words were salves, and rally cries to be brave, the banker call for exchange.

Men who experienced daughters that become wives will tell you,
She's the COIN,
worth the investment.

They'll moan about how if they were disrespectful to her senses or womanhood, how she'd never cheat, for she was invested too, and go on to indicate how they both would seek self-correction, and the offer of correction from one another without nagging. More like a conversation around awareness, where the value is reassessed, and comments are made about the clarity of the diamond or the weight of the gold, the value of negotiation.

Until it is clear a win-win is established. Where discipline and commitment to growth MUST be wrapped around the love all parties are willing to accept.

I mean, honor for heart.

It is two steps forward, 8 steps backwards negotiation so they can reestablish their real desire.

Sex is everywhere.

The law of supply and demand says it is a depreciating fool's gold, not as valuable after it leaves the showroom floor. For no matter how many pumps you perform, when it's over, you must live with yourself.

Man and Woman.

Let us remind EVERYONE, love is sacred.
It's not dates, not gifts, not a warm fuzzy
feeling. It's work, bonding, and
understanding of two lives merging.
You can't bamboozle LOVE.
"Your heart for theirs, make them give it
up or be without you", is not a slogan, but
the password to enter the vault where
value resides.
Teach daughters to have NO problem
walking away.
Let them KNOW ain't no playing allowed
with real money!

Love is real wealth, all else is fallacy.

■■■■■■■■■■■■■■■■■■■■■■■■■■■■■■■■■■
Conversation:
Honoring daughters is not a conversation
around chastity, it is self-discovery and
affirmation of what value is. The culture
of African American society is
overwhelmed by the suggestion that a
woman is only in her prime with she is
attractive to the eyes and displaying the
outward demonstration of the ability to be
fertile, juicy breasts, small waist, and
curves of the hips and thighs. This is not
the only way women can be honorable.

Honorable women reason and establish boundaries for herself, fully aware that someone, a daughter, sister, cousin, niece, or member of the community may see the boundaries and definitions of woman, that SHE has established, and mimic the behaviors that are displayed. Even if they are unaware of the established boundaries and definitions she created. There can be liberation or danger in that approach.

If outward appearance and actions are displayed and never reasoned around, if they lack context of the conversation about why actions, words, or images are displayed, then false, misleading and/or hurtful outcomes may be the result of a very intentional, liberated method of displaying freedom.

You may mean well, but young girls and women create their own ideas about what they see; often using the language given to them by oppression as the context.

Is that what we want?

■■■■■■■■■■■■■■■■■■■■■■■■■■■■■■■■■■■■■■

Action:

Be an appropriate banker of the energy that is YOU. Share the rules, demonstrate your why.

Begin by asking yourself:

Who will I be? What do I WANT to look like? Why do I want to look that way? Who comes closest to my ideal image? What is her story? What will my story be if I choose that path?

Scales of Equality

My thoughts for yours
It used to be normal to hold paper
money to the light to look for the strip of
authenticity, but now stores pull out a
marker to test the science of the paper.
So, it is reasonable that I hold your
currency to a test of realness too, I mean
the thoughts and sounds you make. Not
to belittle you, but so I know you aren't
trying to cheat me.
Put mine on the scales, I offer pure,
unrefined fresh out the mind, mined gold.
Offer me a fair exchange.
One truth of mine, for a truth of yours
and you should know, I don't want pomp
and circumstance of this world.
For trends often determine wealth, I want
what is timeless, I want REAL wealth.
My heart for yours, give it up or be
without me. In all spaces that is the
exchange rate. Don't you know the mind
speaks from the heart?
But me, I'm cautious, I study enough to
know that if I show you my gold, and
you're greedy, even if yours is the same

quality or better, you'll try to rob me of
my goods,
monetize off them, profit with no
consideration of how to grow it is a
RIGHT NOW FIX
mindless, because you are unsure of your
own.
Every mother taught, tuck some coin
away out of sight so you'll survive.
I do that willingly.
I ain't Jack, beans won't do, I'm not
willing to climb any stalk to trick giants
out of their wealth, I understand the soil
is the only real money, for it grew the
stalk...
So, I honor it, knowing I'm made of it...

■■■■■■■■■■■■■■■■■■■■■■■■■■■■■■■■■■■
Conversation:
In this society full of pop-up stores, ideas, trendy new trinkets, be a careful consumer. People will appear to be successful; I mean dressed up in the right clothes to sell you a part of a business, or scheme that makes them rich. It will cause you to abandon your own ideas that came from the heart as worthless. And yes, you may make them money, and get a little money in return, but your own ideas are valuable too! Use your heart and be brave to try and back yourself as you discover what is valuable to YOU. There are adults who have lost all their savings and riches on the promise of an easy dollar. Do your research wherever you give your time or money!

■■■■■■■■■■■■■■■■■■■■■■■■■■■■■■■■■■■

Action:
Be careful of get rich quick schemes. If you have an idea and want to learn from someone else how to make it a reality, there is nothing wrong with learning business structures. Have goals, respect your ideas and don't be afraid of failure.

Begin by asking yourself:
Does this company produce a product? Could I be using money to invest into my own ideas? Is this for the good of the community?

Bring the Ghetto Back to Policy

The most intelligent people called gangster that I ever knew didn't push drugs.

They pushed this system against the wall and got what they needed, and they had big hearts, so they'd turn and say to the person watching their display of power,

"You want something too baby?"

Hair rollers, housecoat, slippers standing face to face with oppression.

But some stayed fly too, I mean with hair done, clothes top of the line, red bottomed shoes clicking in the hallway.

Both types are fierce

Propaganda gave you the old bait and switch, told you that people in the street with guns were the most feared, action driven people that kept the whole block on edge.

Gangster movies, goon series, lyrics about men moving rapid fire off impulse.

They made it seem like the only way to overcome, the one who could get what they want done, but really show of force is the last resort, when words no longer work, and people become desperate. They are the last to move, the forced hand. Shango, Kahli, beings of war who don't care about casualties.

But have you seen a woman fully in her power move? We are not talking rich or poor. We are talking about how, when the sway of hips moves FIRST, most ALWAYS, work gets done.

They have unregistered assault weapons, they flip the switch to burst, loud ricocheting bullets that bounce off what they told you were respectably quiet, oppressive walls

her weapon sounds off loudly, ringing in ears, fully equipped energy of

WORDS

vibrations like,

"Not my baby, where is my husband, you think you can just talk to us like that?"

They make Presidents tremble, and politicians shrink in their suits.

They don't get much airplay though, you have to witness them up close, in the front office of schools, in the back of classrooms, members of PTA sitting ready in school

board meetings, community round tables,
political offices, board room deciders,
standing holding the block up like the
fabled ATLAS

out of sight

but strong arms bracing the load.

Gunshots are often forgotten, but the boom
of her voice makes them write policy to
keep her from rallying her troops, going to
get her family, you know bringing the
whole system down.

They use the power of the pen to appease
her or write rules to keep her out their face.

As a child, I never turned away when
people said she was acting wild.

I stared and thought.

"Why don't we leverage her to our
advantage, so we get what we need?"

Welfare offices, Banks, Schools, at the store,
and on the block with the hood,

EVERYONE shook to their soul when she
got determined.

She is the sure bet.

Leverage our greatest asset, our culture.

It's pure money to utilize the only true OG.

Let her in the room.

She gets things done.

■ ■
Conversation:
I think it is very important that we define
the following words, gangster and ghetto.
According to Merrium-Webster[1]:

Ghetto: 1: a quarter of a city in which Jews were formerly required to
live
2: a quarter of a city in which members of a minority group live
especially because of social, legal, or economic pressure
3 a: an isolated group

Gangster: a member of a gang of criminals

According to the Urban Dictionary[2]:

Ghetto: 1) A run down area of any town or city, but most often used in
terms of the inner city. Any area with low or non-existent property
value. May or may not refer to a high-crime area, but often does.

2) Anything that is jury rigged, broken in some way, or otherwise of
generally poor quality. Refers to the frequency at which poverty-
stricken people must improvise to survive on low income.

Gangster: A gangster is one who participates in organized crime,
typically the Mafia; gangsters commit crimes (killing, gambling, drug
dealing, prostitution) for money.

When defining what to use your voice for,
you must consider the label that others

---

[1] Merriam-Webster: America's Most Trusted
Dictionary
[2] Urban Dictionary, November 25:

have given to you. Labels are often "scare tactics" meant to prevent you from speaking up. They are meant to create fear and shame. Who wants to wear the label "ghetto" or "gangster"? A girl's voice is powerful, and a woman's is more powerful. American culture uses cartoons, movies and shows to paint the picture of black women as loud and out of order. As we define womanhood, consider when to raise our voice and when a soft metered approach will work. If you speak up for the right things, you can help to make the community better. Learn to use your voice. The most dangerous violence is your silence! Speak up for what matters directly to someone who can do something about it!

■ ■

Action:

Take charge of your womanhood by using your words to evoke change:

Begin by asking yourself:

"Will this conversation get the result I need?" "Am I talking to someone who can take action on the words I speak?" Can I unite my voice with other women to make progress?

No Boxes

If you only know me through social media,
you'd have one image, a checkbox of who I
could be based on the things I post. I might
be a totally different person in real life.
You can be anything you want on the
Internet, on social media platforms, in the
digital world.
And if you are easily influenced and not
aware, what is shown in the digital world
will flow into the real world.
But if you are wise, you could use the space
as propaganda of your own. You can shift
the narrative or conversation in your
communities and be a positive or negative
influence.
I remember engaging for a specific task
with a group of people, we only came
together for a specific purpose, in this case
to play sport, I hardly ever spoke. But
people had this tunnel vision of what I
MUST be.
But when I opened up and shared parts of
me, they couldn't imagine, I learned they
built a character in their head and couldn't
accept the duality (the part they imagined
versus the part I explained about myself)

and determined one part couldn't be real,
they chose what script they'd believe.
At my job people have this vision of what I
MUST BE and don't understand why or
how I can know what I know when I reason
with them. I'm trying to tell you, in all
spaces people will TRY to box you in.
And it is really up to you if you'll decide to
get in the box or not.
Boxes don't let light in, they keep it out.
I'm not a character, I AM and YOU ARE a
being. Don't listen to the noise, and don't
become an actor in a script people wrote for
you.
RISE, BE what your soul calls....
You deserve to shine your light
Freely

■■■■■■■■■■■■■■■■■■■■■■■■■■■■■■■■■■■

Conversation:

Social media seems so innocent. But right now, in places like China[3], there are national policies called, "Social Credit" that is being used to determine how you can and will be treated based on your trustworthiness. America is considering something very similar[4]. If a social system is being created, where do you think the information comes from? Will you become or be labeled based on what YOU share of yourself? You may not believe in the MEMEs you post but will they be used against you later?

■■■■■■■■■■■■■■■■■■■■■■■■■■■■■■■■■

---

[3] China invents the digital totalitarian state (economist.com)

[4] Coming soon: America's own social credit system | The Hill

Action:
You are who and what you share on social media, so what story will you tell?

Begin by asking yourself:
Am I upset when I post this? Will it distort who I want to be 5 years from now? If I show pictures of my physical body, will it attract members of the opposite sex to want to take advantage of me? How can I use my post to become the woman I'd like to be?

Be, Will, Grow

Last night I had massive migraines,
light was bothering me so.
But I didn't let it stop me from getting
work done, not to be confused with
resting when needed.
Every single day we are given an
opportunity to BE.
What we choose "to be" is entirely up to
us. I hope I decide daily, every minute, to
show up as
Myself
Honest about what I feel.
vocal about boundaries
aware of perceived limitations
driven about finding new ways to
overcome
But
Persistent in the things
that matter to me
Unrelenting about progress
Aware that
As a woman, I capable of birthing
babies and dreams.
I show and prove,
for myself, and those I adore.
I do it, because I WILL to,

I hope to never give up.
Because I know, my way doesn't have to
be perfect, only an intentional path
towards the light.
Fully aware that my act makes those
around and near me brave to WILL and
"BE" from their heart too.
That's how I grew, someone else turned
on the light for me. May we grow on and
with purpose all days!

■■■■■■■■■■■■■■■■■■■■■■■■■■■■■■■■■■■■
Conversation:

As a girl and woman, you are not going to feel good every single day! Rest when you need to rest, but when you are rejuvenated, get back on your path towards what you are trying do! You get to decide in every single moment what you will do, think and be. It is a privilege to do so.

■■■■■■■■■■■■■■■■■■■■■■■■■■■■■■■■■■■■

Action:
What can you do to maintain your authentic self?

Begin by asking yourself:
How do I feel today? Did I drink enough water? Did I eat properly, including fresh fruit and vegetables? What do I need to do to feel like my best self?

Vision of Fly

I know people are really big on vision
boards. I was never that person.
I was ALWAYS into DATA.
I'd take inventory
of everything I had, everything in my
environment, all the tools at my disposal,
THEN
consider all capabilities, resources, and
opportunities to learn, then finally make a
step-by-step plan.
People, New age thought will tell you
don't think of how to get to where you're
going, but true Alchemy
(creation of gold from nongold things)
requires ACTION,
I mean consistent action of sifting through
the unrefined ingredients, transforming it
to liquid, then applying heat before solid
gold is created.
Vision boards are usually cutouts of what
doesn't belong to you,
a board of envy,
to build hope, all so you get those things
you cut out, with your own hands.
But really, you're touching and agreeing
that you have a lack.

THINK BIGGER
What are your demands- things you need,
what are your soft asks- things you want,
What WILL you?
See the outcome in your mind's eye
and DO THE WORK
As you journey you MUST create with a
pure heart, without envy or jealousy of
what another person has. You HAVE to
shine a light of truth, so your outcomes
can be built on solid ground, the place
where you get pure ingredients, the
consistent place of truth and light.
You'll BE whatever you DO dear souls

■■■■■■■■■■■■■■■■■■■■■■■■■■■■■■■■■■
Conversation:
Creating the life or future you want should never come from a mindset of lack.

You are not creating to be like anyone else or get what anyone else has. That is a poverty mindset. Daughters should define what success looks like for them, and becoming the person they envision can empower the community as well. So, I would caution to not use vision boards that focus on gaining things in this capitalistic American society, but rather creating action plans to be a healthy member of the culture.

■■■■■■■■■■■■■■■■■■■■■■■■■■■■■■■■■■

Action:
What can you do to plan for your future?

Begin by asking yourself:
Why do I want a career? Who said I should have it? Should I get a degree or go to trade school? What must I give up reaching my goal? How will my plan benefit my family and my community?

Money Changer

It's an offense against my soul to be
intentionally mean to other people.
I never liked the way it felt to see
someone shrinking inside the skin that
was gifted to them.
Of all the beautiful things that exist within
humanity, why should I have to look for
one thing wrong with you and leverage it
like a badge of being better than someone
else? It feels like madness to me.
I like looking at people and seeing the
best of them. I enjoy highlighting unique
gifts and becoming your champion. Not
for me, but for some little kid who sees
the outcome and now feels ok about
themselves.
Our culture has a bullying spirit.
The kind that pushes children to suicide,
and forces women to go under the knife to
inject plastic into their bodies, and makes
men floss external gifts, trinkets, THINGS
like they have value.
It's all just so offensive to me
I used to say gossip is a terrorist act
but had to stop, because it might offend
people who like to do it.

I guess they have a right to do it, all I
know is that I just want to guard my
tongue more than I have been.
We use the label narcissism too much, to
cover over the harm bullying does to
people. Sometimes people talk about
their own lives, so they'll never have to
point the finger at anyone else.
I never want to be above anyone; I just
want us all to rise. And every single day I
question how to do that, I don't have all
the answers.
But I know my oddities, my quirky ways,
are the currency given to me since the
start of time. I haven't changed much,
except I try to be a little louder so people
will hear me, but it hurts to strain these
days, it makes me feel weak.
I'm fading back into the background, so I
can do heart work, this loving work and
survive. Because I feel like every
individual's gift being performed from
their heart IS holy work, and I don't want
to prevent anyone else's rise just because
it doesn't look familiar.
Those kinds of thoughts, I mean
consideration of fellow man, are the
greatest money flow, it's the only richness
I know, I mean letting people be

I'm exchanging my coin for yours, adding
water so both our lawns will grow and
there is no reason to envy one another.
It's the only level playing field I can
offer....

▪▪▪▪▪▪▪▪▪▪▪▪▪▪▪▪▪▪▪▪▪▪▪▪▪▪▪▪▪▪▪▪▪▪▪
Conversation:

To change a community or environment
you must change your own mind first.

Be gentle with other people and try not to
bully yourself or others into looking a
certain way, talking, or thinking like
everyone else. Honor differences.

▪▪▪▪▪▪▪▪▪▪▪▪▪▪▪▪▪▪▪▪▪▪▪▪▪▪▪▪▪▪▪▪▪▪▪

Action:
What can you do to support a bully free environment?

Begin by asking yourself:
Did I put my own thoughts of life on that person? Did I give them space to be themselves? Did I laugh at things I didn't understand? Did I seek to understand them?

DNA

I'm always celebrating, revealing what I
see in others. The currency that flows
through their DNA strand.
Yesterday I was called to rise too.
Then the vibration of who IAM was
blessed properly too.
BEING WHO YOU'RE DESIGNED TO BE
that is the only cash money that matters
on this plane of existence.

■■■■■■■■■■■■■■■■■■■■■■■■■■■■■■■■■
Conversation:
Can you honor yourself and others for
being exactly what they are made of?

Hair, Eyes, Body, and skin are designed.
Celebrate the genius of your DNA.
Celebrate the creation of others too.

■■■■■■■■■■■■■■■■■■■■■■■■■■■■■■■■■

Action:

Feel comfortable in your genetic makeup and make others feel comfortable in theirs too.

Begin by asking yourself:

Do I show joy of my design? Do I show joy in the design of others?

High Dollar Words

Before texting became popular, I used to
have a beeper. A tiny black box with
Minnie Mouse on the cover.
I'm not much of a face-to-face talker
but I loved leaving messages on other
people's voicemail and finding treasures
on mine.
I'd express love, tell people I was thinking
of them, or simply say hi.
I received just as many messages as I
gave.

Before beepers became popular, I used to
buy pretty stationery. My favorite
happened to be a white pad with pink
flowers all around the edge. I'm not much
of a face-to-face talker
but I loved leaving notes on other people's
property and have them find the treasure.
Some wrote me back, on ordinary lined
paper, but a letter just the same.
I'd express my fears, tell about the light I
see, or simply make them smile.

Before stationery was popular or
obtainable, I used to smile real big and let

people hug me. I'm not much of a face-to-face talker.

But my favorite hugs happened to be from my Big Daddy (Grandfather), cause he'd tap my back and say it's alright girl, I'm happy to see you.

I'd sink in the safety, and never had to express a thing, for his arms were a reset button.

Quiet peace.

I'm trying to tell you something.

Communication has evolved, but expression has not.

So, I'll remind you, hate, anger, rage, are things that belong outside of you, not in you, and that when you vibrate towards other people I hope you'll speak of love, power, encouragement, and joy.

Because love energy DOES belong in you and around you, for it was here in the beginning, and it's the only REAL dollar.

So, use your communication of words wisely...

■■■■■■■■■■■■■■■■■■■■■■■■■■■■■■■■■■
Conversation:

Can you image if you were paid from the words you speak, use, or give to others in all formats?

I think it is so important to consider that every sound and vibration creates something. So, the energy that young women say word or elder women can be considered a currency. Do you remember what happened when someone said words that made your heart happy? Now think about what happened when someone said words that made your heart sad. Sometimes it can be the same words given at different times but landing on you when you are not in the best of moods. Emotion filled words are very costly, and you can't take them back. Remember words cost something, to the giver and receiver!

■■■■■■■■■■■■■■■■■■■■■■■■■■■■■■■■■■

Action:
Compliment generously and give correction with the same generosity. Remembering that both expressions create something in another person.

Begin by asking yourself:
Is my conversation necessary? Am I giving words that help or harm? Can the conversation wait until I am less emotional and can use my words with intention?

Mind Exchange

All money has an exchange rate.
During slavery, your physical self was the
coin, the individual person could be
placed on an auction block in exchange
for money.
In this new slavery, there are segments of
the population that STILL ARE the
coin. The individual is watched for a
violation against laws they didn't help
write, on a judge's auction block, time
exchanged to the industrial complex.
But on the spiritual plane, the individual
makes a CHOICE to become a slave,
based on the information they place
before their physical bodies. The currency
buys a ticket to heaven or hell, a dwelling
place from which there is no escape,
inside your thoughts.
Whatever happens on this earth, you are
in control of the only real money all
slavers seek to leverage for their gain...
YOUR MIND
Control your block dear souls

■■■■■■■■■■■■■■■■■■■■■■■■■■■■■■■■■■

Conversation:

I think so often we make people unapproachable because of the money they make, the title they carry, the unreal, manmade cost we put on people's time and energy. Then we let others place a price tag on us. You are not anyone's slave. You are not on an auction block, you have your freedom, what is your rate?

■■■■■■■■■■■■■■■■■■■■■■■■■■■■■■■■■■

Action:

You determine your cost in all spaces.

Begin by asking yourself:

What is my cost? If I had to charge someone by the hour for my time, what would I say I was worth? Do I have a fair exchange rate? Am I not a human too? What and where will I exchange my energy for resources? Whose exchange rate do I use, mine or theirs?

Adopted Language

I didn't ask to be a "Baby Momma" I
intended; I was groomed to be a WIFE.
But I made choices and when I manifested
a LIFE without a ring
I did what ANYONE without a diamond
shining, could CHOOSE to do
I looked at the stats, studied my options
and mapped a plan for my DNA strand.
While I began in collaboration, I ended
going solo down this path...
One of poverty, in mind and dollars
But shoulders heavy carrying the weight
of someone's else's words of demise
"Baby Mommas ruin the community and
are an unsavory part of the black
experience" one where the system creates
a path, where everyone else abandons
you, the path given is called "Poverty"
And everyone, all people know, poverty
is sometimes a death sentence if you don't
know a way out...one with generational
consequences.
I did not adopt their language
I politely rejected it.
Instead, I USED all resources available,
sacrificed, spent time at the library, went

to court when reason couldn't be received
and STOOD chest out shouting...
I CHOOSE LIFE, not just any life
A GOOD LIFE judged on my standards
for MY PARTIAL, but REALLY my whole
RESPONSIBILITY
FOR THIS CHILD
Will have options, beyond the poverty
offered to me as a quick, easy way out...
I took a new language, one I learned in
books and lectures, I applied the concepts,
I saw the light and I educated the
darkness away...still aware...fully
afraid...but eyes towards his future...
I'm NOT what they told you IAM
Vowels, and Consonants
Rearranged to create my own sound, but
really the revival of an old tongue:
BE FRUITFUL and MULTIPLY
A gift, with unlimited options available
I was groomed to be a WIFE.
So, I did what wives do, help the family
thrive

****

Conversation:

Words mean something, they come with background ideas and can be a curse or a form of liberation. Don't you know even in fortune telling, the future can be changed?

Abstinence is a powerful decision to make as you venture into adulthood and seek a partner, but should you create an outcome that doesn't align don't adopt someone's decision about how your life should turn out.
■■■■■■■■■■■■■■■■■■■■■■■■■■■■■■■■■■

Action:

Learn words, learn ways to use them to create the life you want.

Begin by asking yourself:

Is there another way? Who overcame this obstacle before me? What tools did they use? What can happen if I choose this direction? Years will pass by; how can I make the future a comfortable experience? Can I go to school? Should I fill out the FAFSA? Does it cost more to work, or does it cost more to NOT learn? Can I be uncomfortable for a little while to be comfortable for years to come?

Alchemy of Energy

Once you know who you are, you'd NEVER
seek to believe the hype this world tries to
feed you...

Alchemy is the ability to change normal
everyday things into melanin rich gold
As an ALCHEMIST, I happen to know that
you MUST revisit history.
Revisiting gives insight, I mean the root,
original design of a situation, or the first
occurrence of a problem if one exists.
Because sometimes we SEE the NOW, the
real thing that exists, the tangible we can
touch and see, forgetting it was created
upon a foundation.
Sometimes foundations are weak and
MUST be reinforced, I mean strengthening
the weak areas, or if it is too damaged, a
restart must happen...
While things exist in this world, we are
visitors, so don't let trinkets distract, don't
get that confused with meeting certain
benchmarks to creation. The final goal of
alchemy is discovery, of self and
environment.
Getting degrees, promotions, having people
speak of loving you.

Are all a part of the process, NEEDED
milestones on the way, the fire to heat the
materials to form the gold.
Intellectual minds must be challenged,
dollars must be earned, and hearts MUST
have a reason to beat.
Each phase requires focus.
So, when witnessing other people
journeying, why shouldn't we make life
easier for them? I mean can't we be a water
break on their marathon?
As an ALCHEMIST you CAN change the
environment, and sometimes that requires
force, but sometimes it is a soft polishing of
the final product of gold. I pray we know
which is which.
All the while knowing that deen is a way of
life, not subject to be below ANY man-made
laws.
You are not what they told you, IAM is
light, divided into fragments, shining
within you, when you created your strong
foundation, you put yours on the table and
help us light our way. Your Alchemy
matters.

****

Conversation:

There is nothing new under that sun. Every action came from somewhere, and everything we create is built on a foundation. This is where the idea of generational blessings or curses come from. But what if we consider getting to the origin of behavior information to create the" GOLD" of life that we have been looking for?

▪▪▪▪▪▪▪▪▪▪▪▪▪▪▪▪▪▪▪▪▪▪▪▪▪▪▪▪▪▪▪▪▪▪

Action:

Learn to start at the beginning when you are trying to change anything!

Begin by asking yourself:

What happened, who was involved, was love involved, or was this behavior or space built out of a need to protect? Was the behavior, thing, or place the result of anger? What tools did they use? Were groups involved? Did an individual leader guide the space?

Don't Blow my Flame Out

I have been doing my work, but it seems
like the Universe always wants to see how
I'll apply lessons under pressure.
It is like taking your lit flame and walking
outside with it, pure exposure.
I can tell you, being worried about how
someone looks at you often keeps us in a
state of fear, protecting, covering the light
from being blown out.
It is a hostage situation where you're in
false love with a "WILL" a reality, outside
of your own, an oppressive force...
when really, you're in hate/mistrust of
self
Afraid of saying "No" I won't, or "No"
don't, the needed cupped hands around a
flame to keep the fire going. And I know,
using "No" feels like guilt, a suppression
of your own will, pure worry about how
it is received.
But, after many times of having my flame
blown out.
And the price I had to pay to reignite my
flame...

I don't feel guilty anymore.
I stand my ground.
I don't let anyone else hold me hostage to their WILL.
I have a choice on what I want to experience in life.
My "Yes" and "No" unlock my journey.
"NO" is the greatest gift ever given to you. Its twin is, "Stop that I don't like that." Its polite Mother is,
"NO THANK YOU."
They are the glass you put around your light to keep the flame bright when you step out into the elements.
Use THEM

****

Conversation:

The work you do on yourself is taxing and full of twists and turns. In a community of "US" you must do what is for the good of the whole, but not at the expense of your own light. Learn to give of self without tearing chunks away that you need to survive.

■■■■■■■■■■■■■■■■■■■■■■■■■■■■■■■■■■■■

Action:

Learn the power of your "yes" and "no". Those tiny words make a major impact on your wellbeing. They are the difference between maintaining a lit flame or putting it out yourself. Because you should never forget that your decision is YOUR action, and you live with the outcome.

Begin by asking yourself:

What must I give up by saying, "Yes"? What must I give up by saying, "No"? Then determine if your community is diminished or empowered through your action. Will YOU suffer, will your family suffer, will you be able to give the best, whole of yourself if you use the sound of your own voice to blow out your flame, with the action that you take.

Generational Lights

By participating in book clubs, you find out the way peers, elders, and youth think. For example, in one book club space, it was expressed that elders are frustrated with the youth because they don't obey authority.

I had this to say, and I have said it in multiple spaces....

"Our youth SHOULD challenge the system. If you're not going to teach them how that should happen, then we must close our mouths when they do it their way. They don't want, nor should they have to be docile and make no noise because it makes you uncomfortable."

Every single society's revolution is fought by YOUTH. They are on the ground and have no money or resources to run to safe spaces. They ARE the front line.

Step up and teach them how to manage their light...or you'll taint the balanced voice we need. We need soft, AND loud to get to where we are trying to go.

You want to be free or not?

****

Conversation:

We must learn to communicate and teach our youth how to use their flames, I mean their passion to promote change, or they will do it their way.

■■■■■■■■■■■■■■■■■■■■■■■■■■■■■■■■■■■

Action:

When creating rules at home, policy in state and federal spaces, ask for a cross-section of youth to provide their voice.

Begin by asking yourself:
Did I make space for younger generations to be heard? Am I forcing the ideas of one generation on to the next? Can I provide space, time, and intentionality behind hearing their voice in non-emergency situations?

Numbers Game

There are sons who are sooooo brilliant,
that numbers absorb like rain in a parched
desert. They soak it all in. Some
daughters too...
And if given the chance, they'd focus on
the many variations, variables, all day
every day.
But they get snagged up in the illogical
words of the human language. They can't
explain how they know what they know,
just that they know. So, language
becomes the tool "educators", social
conditioners use to bury their gift.
It sounds like, "Do this my way for your
way isn't, can't be real, because college
didn't teach me to teach it to you that
way."
And slowly we lose them down the tube
of embarrassment. Shame. Because
they're told that to do it in their head
means they do it wrong or they
cheated. Or to do it in a way not familiar,
means they are not smart, when neatly
ordered readable rows simply mean that
they are just obedient like the others.

So, the numbers grow silent, and they no
longer talk that special language to
themselves anymore.
You should know, some lights are put out
because the flame doesn't look
familiar...when it could be the new way,
we all need.
Some hustlers aren't on the street corners,
they drive policy that kills intellect

****

Conversation:

Can you imagine the brilliance that is stifled because we don't perform in life the way others want us to?

■ ■

Action:

Even if you don't have language to explain your why, never let go of that thing you do naturally.

Begin by asking yourself:

Could this thing I do be a gift? How can I continue to practice it? Can I research more about it? Can I use social media to connect with people beyond my community?

Books to Grow

I love reading Paulo Coelho because I
know he took mysticism and turned the
key themes into a storyline. Octavia
Butler happened to be a soothsayer in all
her works...a channel.
I think the translation of spiritual things
into the ordinary everyday application is
a beautiful thing.
I mean taking the essence of the Highest
Frequency and making it physically a
touchable entity for everyone.
I love reading, but I love even more
people who embody the lessons.
They make me feel brave to conquer this
life. They are the totem poles Natives
build, the High Priest in jeans, and the
Wise Sage on the mountain, here on our
blocks....
Prophets are everyday ordinary Moms,
Dads, strangers, that little kid asking the
right question...
I have learned that righteousness rides a
frequency, it's light travel...
pay attention
or you'll miss the characters coming to life

****

Conversation:

Every writer is a person that is crafting an experience for the reader. Think of it like the Matrix where you need to upload information to perform a new task. Books have the capacity to empower you. Don't be biased when it comes to choosing your books, expand your mind through new words, ideas, and cultures.

■■■■■■■■■■■■■■■■■■■■■■■■■■■■■■■■■■■

Action:

It is important that you read stories, physical books and digital books that take your mind on a ride beyond the stories and engagement you are used to.

Begin by asking yourself:

What piques my interest? What would I like to learn? Do I need a storyline with actions? Do I need a serious instructional space? How can the arrangement of words in this book help me in the world?

Labor Pains

Last week, a major project I spearheaded, after months of research and planning, was close to being tanked. I felt defeated, my career and reputation being drug carelessly. My seat at the table, which already had bent legs, forcing me to stand, was giving me the blues.
It was a relationship problem. They couldn't see the human in me.
But Monday, yesterday, and today...I hyped my ego, held my head up, and straightened my back...to prep myself to sit down with confidence.
A room full of "no", "we can't do that" people. I had to sell them my vision. 10 minutes, that's all I had, and 2 of them were taken for introductions.
But for one of those minutes, a man told the whole room, "This is LaShonda's brainchild. A strategic engagement not ever performed here, the first of its kind and I'm amazed at the thought and future vision put into it."

Then I lit into my well researched facts,
projected outcomes, and pitch for the
GREATEST GOOD.
It was accepted without objection, an ask
that helps everyone, but removes long
standing institutionalized biases.
Tomorrow, the system may punish me for
the outcome. But today, I breathe,
preparing for a moment of relax....
I prepare my spirit for what's next.
I'm not different, I just don't give up. I
approach problems from multiple angles
because there's an opening somewhere in
this oppressive system. My Ancestors
walking through the back door, or side
entrance, taught me to check all the doors,
knowing that one of them will let you in
the room, to petition for what you need
too.
The harder work begins tomorrow, but
today...I birthed my baby, and it is full of
life...some call it light...
I'm saying my gratitude for divine
covering and guidance....

****

Conversation:

Every writer is a person that is crafting an experience for the reader. Consider, in the Matrix, information was uploaded to learn a new task. Books, presentations, sharing of ideas have the capacity to empower you like that. The process is like a baby in womb, you research needs, nourish the creation by reading to it, then create an optimal space for it to come alive and grow. You must appeal to cultures outside of your own if you want the baby you are bringing forth to survive. So, don't be biased when it comes to choosing your books, expand your mind through new words, ideas, and cultures.

■■■■■■■■■■■■■■■■■■■■■■■■■■■■■■■■■■■■■

Action:

Not everything you try or want, can be done alone. Sometimes you MUST have allies.

Begin by asking yourself:

Who is best suited to carry this message? Will this help advance humanity? Am I willing to give the thing created over, to advance the greater mission, seeking nothing but better outcomes "for the PEOPLE" in return? Does it matter who gets credit as long as the community benefits? Learn to give things up to win. But most importantly learn to SPEAK up when given the opportunity.

Old Money

At the decision table, I'm bold, and I'm
not easily shaken, because I come
PREPARED; facts, stats, past behavior,
and expected outcomes strategized.

I sit dressed in all the losses, all the wins
my people experienced. I had to LIVE
through them, so when I speak, it is the
MATTER OF FACTS, not opinions.
But I'm also aware, everything doesn't
work everywhere. Attitudes, experience,
and confidence make a difference, mine
and the intended receiver of my message.
I'm not one to sell ANYONE something
they don't need or want.
I'm not jazzing myself up to distract you, I
want you to hear me in my plainness
my original being
for my foundation is solid
I say, "I did an assessment, I think I
understand what you seek, here are some
options to get you there" fully aware that
decisions are in the hands of the receiver
of the message

I'm only trying to share what was gifted to me and receive what you're willing to give. All my dealings are fair exchanges. I've been called a hidden jewel for my effort.

I never force, you may never even hear my voice if my Ancestors, elders, intuition tell me not to engage you...and you should know, there are some they love more than others and will try to redeem over and over again for all our good.   Especially those they KNOW will run from their calling....

They have a RIGHT, a WILL to reject the calling

But me, I'm ALWAYS WILLING to receive and act...for I am always about my FATHER'S business...the Ancestors, elders, spirit, my intuition stand around me like I'm the bride, showering money...like life is a wedding and they want to bless me, equip me to bring the trophy home...they know I'll bring it home...they call me a beloved daughter, because I'm obedient to Universal Laws. YOU HAVE TO GET OBEDIENT TO RECEIVE, they test and try you...losses and wins...so they understand your character...I've been through the flames, and they KNOW, I submit willingly...

My ignorance for their wisdom, that's the
only real money.
****

The final prose of this book ends with no conversation or action within the book, because it is time for you think, plan, and act.

Dear Child of the CULTURE, as a daughter of the culture, I can attest, this is a choose your own "WILLED" adventure, called life.

If the old way of the world is not working for you. Maybe it is time to build a new way. The next section of this book is for YOU, write your way to freedom.

I hope you take something from the lessons of this work and build the life you desire. Family cycles, labels, and whatever is called currency today, coin is not the wealth to build the life you want. Your "WILL" is. Your "Will" is your desire, that turns into an action. You CAN be, do, and have a comfortable life, however you define that, it is your mind, your imagination. Dream BIG.

Love,

LaShonda

Free Write a poem or prose:

Use this space to explain your poem:

What action will you take?

Use your imagination, write your ideal state. Now write an action to help you work to become what you imagine:

Idea	Action to take
Ex. I want to know more about Information Technology	Ex. I will take a Coursera course or take free trainings on YouTube.

Free Write a poem or prose:

Use this space to explain your poem:

What action will you take?

Use your imagination, write your ideal state. Now write an action to help you work to become what you imagine:

Idea	Action to take
Ex. I want to learn to paint.	Ex. I will find free classes in my area.

Free Write a poem or prose:

Use this space to explain your poem:

What action will you take?

Use your imagination, write your ideal state. Now write an action to help you work to become what you imagine:

Idea	Action to take
Ex. I want to be fit.	I will work out 3 times a week.

Free Write a poem or prose:

Use this space to explain your poem:

What action will you take?

Use your imagination, write your ideal state. Now write an action to help you work to become what you imagine:

Idea	Action to take
Ex. I want to learn a new language.	Ex. I will join a community that practices speaking this language.

Free Write a poem or prose:

Use this space to explain your poem:

What action will you take?

Use your imagination, write your ideal state. Now write an action to help you work to become what you imagine:

Idea	Action to take
Ex. I want to be a better friend.	Ex. Be a person people can call friendly.

Free Write a poem or prose:

Use this space to explain your poem:

What action will you take?

Use your imagination, write your ideal state. Now write an action to help you work to become what you imagine:

Idea	Action to take

Free Write a poem or prose:

Use this space to explain your poem:

What action will you take?

Use your imagination, write your ideal state. Now write an action to help you work to become what you imagine:

Idea	Action to take

Free Write a poem or prose:

Use this space to explain your poem:

What action will you take?

Use your imagination, write your ideal state. Now write an action to help you work to become what you imagine:

Idea	Action to take

Free Write a poem or prose:

Use this space to explain your poem:

What action will you take?

Use your imagination, write your ideal state. Now write an action to help you work to become what you imagine:

Idea	Action to take

Free Write a poem or prose:

_____

_____

_____

_____

_____

Use this space to explain your poem:

_____

_____

_____

_____

_____

What action will you take?

_____

_____

_____

_____

_____

Use your imagination, write your ideal state. Now write an action to help you work to become what you imagine:

Idea	Action to take

Free Write a poem or prose:

Use this space to explain your poem:

What action will you take?

Use your imagination, write your ideal state. Now write an action to help you work to become what you imagine:

Idea	Action to take

Free Write a poem or prose:

Use this space to explain your poem:

What action will you take?

Use your imagination, write your ideal state. Now write an action to help you work to become what you imagine:

Idea	Action to take

Free Write a poem or prose:

Use this space to explain your poem:

What action will you take?

Use your imagination, write your ideal state. Now write an action to help you work to become what you imagine:

Idea	Action to take

This Page Left Intentionally Blank to make room for your Growth.